MAY 28 2014

D1273833

Restaurant Owners

Guest Check

BY CECILIA MINDEN AND MARY MINDEN-ZINS

The Child's World

Published by The Child's World®
1980 Lookout Drive • Mankato, MN 56003-1705
800-599-READ • www.childsworld.com

Acknowledgments
The Child's World®: Mary Berendes, Publishing Director
The Design Lab: Design
Jody Jensen Shaffer: Editing
Pamela J. Mitsakos: Photo Research

Photos
asiseeit/iStock.com: 5; BrandXPictures: garlic,
guest check; Dmitry Kalinovsky/Shutterstock.com:
cover, 1; Imageegami/Dreamstime.com: 6-7; Ingrid
Balabanova/Shutterstock.com: 22; Jupiterimages/
Thinkstock.com: 8; Linda M. Armantrout: 9. 19;
Photodisc: design elements; Silberkorn/iStock.com: 17;
Tatyana Gladskikh/Dreamstime.com: 20-21; vitranc/
iStock.com: 4; YinYang: 10-11; yraffah/iStock.com: 14

ISBN 9781626870178
LCCN 2013947294

Printed in the United States of America
Mankato, MN
December, 2013
PA02191

ABOUT THE AUTHORS

Dr. Cecilia Minden is a university professor and reading specialist with classroom and administrative experience in grades K–12. She earned her PhD in reading education from the University of Virginia.

Mary Minden-Zins is an experienced classroom teacher. She taught first grade for ten years before taking time out to raise her children and grandchildren. Mary now teaches kindergarten and lives in Oklahoma.

CONTENTS

Hello, My Name Is Anna.

Hello. My name is Anna. Many people live and work in my neighborhood. Each of them helps the neighborhood in different ways.

I thought of all the things I like to do. I like helping my family cook in the kitchen. I am good at working with numbers. I like helping people come together to have a good time. How could I help my neighborhood when I grow up?

I Could Be a Restaurant Owner!

Restaurant owners help think up yummy dishes for their customers to try. They know a lot about food, and they are good at keeping track of money. Best of all, restaurant owners help bring families and friends together over a delicious meal!

Restaurant owners need to know what foods their customers like.

Learn About This Neighborhood Helper!

The best way to learn is to ask questions. Words such as *who*, *what*, *where*, *when*, and *why* will help me learn about being a restaurant owner.

Where Can I Learn More?
National Restaurant Association
1200 17th Street NW
Washington, DC 20036

Women Chefs and Restaurateurs
304 W. Liberty Street, Suite 201
Louisville, KY 40202

Asking a restaurant owner questions will help you learn more about the job.

Who Can Become a Restaurant Owner?

Boys and girls who like helping their families cook may want to become restaurant owners. Restaurant owners also must be organized and have good math skills. They need to understand how to make money and spend it wisely.

How Can I Explore This Job?

Ask to speak to the owner the next time you eat at a restaurant. Find out what he likes best about his job. What is the hardest part of owning a restaurant? What are some of his biggest responsibilities?

Restaurant owners are important neighborhood helpers. They give people a place to enjoy a good meal. Many restaurant owners even help feed the poor in their neighborhood.

Restaurant owners have to make important decisions about money for their business to do well.

Meet a Restaurant Owner!

This is Glen Armantrout. Glen is one of the owners of a restaurant in New Orleans, Louisiana, called the Acme Oyster House. His restaurant is part of a **chain**.

Glen also works as a restaurant operator. This means he is in charge of making sure all the restaurants in the chain are doing a good job.

Glen owns an Acme Oyster House in New Orleans.

Some restaurants are fancy. Some feel more like home.

Where Can I Learn to Be a Restaurant Owner?

Many people who own restaurants start off doing other jobs in the restaurant business. Glen's first job was washing dishes in a restaurant. He later learned new skills and was able to take different jobs.

People who want to be restaurant owners often take classes in college. They need to be good at math so they can work with money and a **budget**. Restaurant owners may take special business classes to learn these skills. They often get a degree in restaurant management.

Some restaurant owners take classes at cooking schools. They learn how different foods are prepared. It is important for restaurant owners to know about all the different parts of the business.

What Does a Restaurant Owner Need to Do the Job?

Restaurants have many different workers. Glen works with cooks, servers, hostesses, dishwashers, and **managers**. He has to make sure that everyone has the supplies they need to do their jobs. Some of these supplies include pots, pans, trays, plates, silverware, napkins, and menus.

What Are Some Tools I Will Use?
- Calculator
- Cell phone
- Computer
- Fax machine

What Clothes Will I Wear?

For men:
- Dress jacket
- Dress shirt
- Slacks

For women:
- Dress
- Pantsuit

Both men and women wear a hairnet and/or rubber gloves when they're in areas where food is prepared.

Like many restaurant owners, Glen uses his cell phone to order the supplies he needs. He uses his computer to keep track of the **inventory** and the number of customers who eat at his restaurant. Glen's computer also helps him work on the budget and record decisions about money.

Restaurant owners talk to suppliers of goods for their restaurant.

Where Does a Restaurant Owner Work?

There are special names for the different parts of a restaurant. The front of the house is where the customers eat their food. The back of the house includes the kitchen, where the food is prepared. The kitchen is also sometimes called the heart of the house because it is where all the cooking takes place.

Most restaurants also have an office in the back of the house. The office usually has computer, a telephone, file cabinet, and a

What's It Like Where I'll Work?

Restaurants are busy places. Fast-food restaurants may be less fancy than certain sit-down restaurants. Both types of restaurants usually have several different workers who are all moving quickly. Most restaurant owners divide their time between an office and the front of the house. It is important that restaurants are kept very clean so that workers and diners stay healthy!

place to keep notes. This is where a restaurant owner runs the business.

Glen usually gets to work early in the morning. He spends some of his time at the front of the house talking to customers. Glen also does a lot of work in his office.

Sometimes Glen visits other restaurants. He goes to meetings and helps plan how Acme Oyster House restaurants can do the best job possible for their customers.

How Much Money Will I Make?
Most restaurant owners make between $50,000 and $63,500 a year. (These numbers may vary depending on what type of restaurant a person owns.)

Glen spends some of his time working with other Acme Oyster House owners.

Who Works with Restaurant Owners?

Sixty employees work at Glen's restaurant. Each one has an important job. The cooks, dishwashers, hosts, managers, and servers all work together to keep the customers happy. Glen helps make sure that these workers have everything they need to do the best job they can. He also has help from Mike Rodrigue, the other owner of the restaurant.

What other Jobs Might I Like?
- Food inspector
- Grocery store manager or owner
- Hotel manager or owner

Most restaurants have many different workers. Each one plays an important role in keeping customers happy.

When Is a Restaurant Owner a Magician?

Acme Oyster House restaurants are famous for serving oysters. Oysters belong to the same group of animals as clams and snails. Acme Oyster House restaurants serve more than 4 million raw oysters each year.

A hard shell covers the oyster. People open the oyster by shucking off, or removing, the shell. It takes practice to be an expert at shucking oysters. Sometimes lucky diners open the oyster and, like magic, they find a pearl inside!

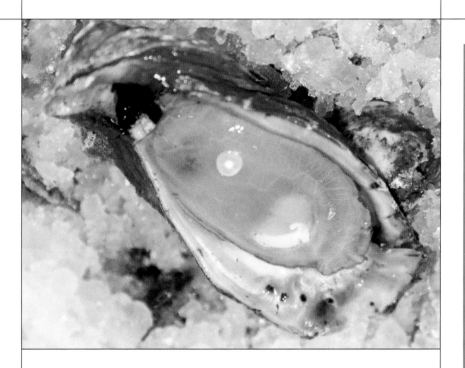

Does the restaurant put the pearl there? No! Oysters make the pearls themselves. But Glen and other restaurant owners make the decision to serve oysters. They play a big part in helping some happy customers walk away with a pearl!

Have you ever tried eating an oyster?
Perhaps you'll be lucky and will find a pearl inside!

I Want to Be a Restaurant Owner!

I think being a restaurant owner would be a great way to be a neighborhood helper. Someday you may be eating a meal in my restaurant!

Is This Job Growing?
The need for restaurant owners will grow more than other jobs.

Maybe one day you'll provide your neighborhood with tasty food and a fun place to eat.

Why Don't You Try Being a Restaurant Owner?

Do you think you would like to be a restaurant owner? It's good for a restaurant owner to know how to prepare and serve food. Work with an adult to make a simple meal for your family. Volunteer to help serve this meal.

You can even decorate the table with colorful place mats made from construction paper.

It's helpful for restaurant owners to know how to prepare different foods.

GLOSSARY

budget (BUJ-et) a plan for how to spend a certain amount of money over a certain period of time

chain (CHAYN) restaurants in different locations that share a common name, menu, and look

inventory (IN-ven-tor-ee) a list of the amounts of various goods that a restaurant has on hand

managers (MAN-uh-jurz) people who direct other workers and watch over their activities

LEARN MORE ABOUT RESTAURANT OWNERS

BOOKS

Duvall, Jill D. *Chef Ki Is Serving Dinner!* Danbury, CT: Children's Press, 1997.

Radabaugh, Melinda Beth. *Going to a Restaurant*. Chicago: Heinemann Library, 2003.

Schaefer, Lola M. *Fast-Food Restaurant*. Chicago: Heinemann Library, 2001.

WEB SITES

Visit our home page for lots of links about restaurant owners:

www.childsworld.com/links

Note to Parents, Teachers, and Librarians: We routinely check our Web links to make sure they're safe, active sites—so encourage your readers to check them out!

INDEX